WE WERE HERE FIRST
THE NATIVE AMERICANS

THE
CHOCTAW

Tamra B. Orr

PURPLE TOAD
PUBLISHING

WE WERE HERE FIRST
THE NATIVE AMERICANS

The Apache of the Southwest
The Blackfeet
The Cherokee
The Cheyenne
The Choctaw
The Comanche
The Creek
The Inuit of the Arctic
The Iroquois of the Northeast
The Lenape
The Navajo
The Nez Perce of the Pacific Northwest
The Seminole
The Sioux of the Great Northern Plains
The Zuni

Printing   1   2   3   4   5   6   7   8   9

Publisher's Cataloging-in-Publication Data
Orr, Tamra B.
    Choctaw / written by Tamra B. Orr.
       p. cm.
Includes bibliographic references, glossary, and index.
    ISBN 9781624693144
1. Choctaw Indians-- Juvenile literature. 2. Indians of North America--Southern States--Juvenile literature. I. Series: We Were Here First: The Native Americans.
    E99.C8 2017
    976.00497
Library of Congress Control Number: 2016957435

eBook ISBN: 9781624693151

CONTENTS

Small stalks of young corn attract hungry crows. The corn has to be watched and protected from these birds and other animals.

CHAPTER 1
WATCHING AND WAITING

The sun's rays spilled across the young fields. Long rows of green sprouts were poking from the dirt, a promise of the cornstalks they would turn into later that summer. A slight breeze ruffled the plants and helped to cool the sweat on Talako's forehead. He felt his eyes grow heavy in the afternoon heat.

No! Talako shook his head and sat up straighter. He could not fall asleep. He had a job to do! Everyone in the family did. His big sister Paloma collected firewood and water. Opa combed the forest for nuts, fruit, and berries. In the afternoons, Talako's father sent his youngest son to keep a close eye on the fields. Each corn plant was precious to the tribe, so each had to be carefully protected. Talako was proud of his job, as he knew it helped his village.

Shading his eyes, the young Choctaw boy watched for any sign of hungry squirrels or raccoons that might munch on the delicate corn shoots. Talako also looked up, knowing that another threat came from black crows. They would fly down to feast on a few seeds or tender leaves for lunch.

Blowgun hunting was a skill that required patience and practice. It was the perfect way to hunt quietly, but accurately.

Just as Talako began to notice his eyelids growing heavy again, a rabbit wandered into the field. Slowly, so slowly the birds did not even quit their singing, Talako raised his *uski hlumpa*, or blowgun, to his lips. The blowgun was longer than he was tall. Loaded in the end of it was a *shumo holutti*, or sharp dart.[1] The blowgun was made from a long, hollow piece of river cane, which is a type of bamboo. This important plant grew near creeks, rivers, and swamps. The Choctaw people used it to make many items, including fishing poles, baskets, mats, and pots.

Talako loved his blowgun and took good care of it. His older brother, Shikoba, had made it for him. Slowly and carefully, Shikoba had held each part of the long piece of cane over hot coals. This softened the length of cane and made it easier to straighten. Then, the young man had picked up another piece of river cane with a sharpened end. He pushed it through

Types of blowgun darts

6

the straightened piece to make sure the blowgun was smooth and hollow inside, from one end to the other. Any bumps or rough spots would make it harder to use. Finally, the brothers had worked to make darts from sharpened pieces of wood.[2]

Shikoba's blowgun was much bigger than Talako's. It was seven feet long, and its darts were almost two feet long. Shikoba used his weapon on hunting trips with the other men. He had used it to kill small game, such as squirrels and raccoons. He knew how to recognize the tracks of many different animals, and his aim was close to perfect. No wonder some of the white men referred to the Choctaws' blowguns as "the breath of death." One day, when both boys were older and more skilled, they would put down their blowguns. They would replace them with the more traditional and effective bows and arrows the men used to hunt.[3]

Holding the end of the blowgun to his mouth, Talako blew into it quickly and firmly. It made a soft coughing sound. The dart flew through the air and would have hit the invading rabbit if the creature had not jumped away at the last second. Talako was disappointed. He had missed! He had hoped to bring a rabbit home for dinner.

Rabbits were a main source of food for the Choctaw—when the animals didn't jump away too fast.

7

Although the bunaha took time to make, it was one of the most commonly eaten foods for the Choctaw. It made great use of the corn husks pulled off during harvest time. They were the perfect wrappers!

Ah well, he thought. At least he had protected the baby corn plants. Now they would have a better chance to grow tall. The ears of sweet corn would be harvested and then turned into one of his mother's wonderful *bunaha*. These dumplings were made with cornmeal and boiled beans. His mother would wrap them in cornhusks and set them near the fire to steam. Talako could not wait to eat them. They were his favorite snack. His mouth was already watering, even though the treat was still months away.

Talako shook his head once again. He could not let his mind wander. He had an important job to do. Once again, he sat up straight and scanned the field for any invaders. He would do everything he could to protect the crop—and try not to daydream about those delicious dumplings.

The Choctaw Language

The Choctaw language is very similar to other Indian languages from the same area, including the Cherokee and the Chickasaw. Here are some of their most common words:[4]

English	Choctaw
One	Achaffa
Two	Tuklo
Three	Tuchena
Four	Ushta
Five	Talhapi
Man	Hattak
Woman	Ohoyo
Dog	Ofi
Sun	Hvshi
Moon	Hvshi
Water	Oka
White	Hanta *or* Tohbi
Yellow	Lvkna
Red	Humma
Black	Lusa
Eat	Vpa
See	Pisa
Hear	Haklo
Sing	Taloa
Leave	Filvmmi *or* Issa

A Choctaw village, as seen in this painting by François Bernard, was a busy place. Each person had a job to do.

CHAPTER 2
FROM CORN TO CATTLE

The earliest days of the Choctaw focused on one thing: moving around to find new supplies of food. They moved constantly, following food sources. This nomadic lifestyle was guided by the seasons. Spring and summer gave them plenty of wild plants and game. In autumn and winter, food was scarce. The tribe had to keep on the move to find enough fresh food to survive until the sun's warmth returned.

Around 900 CE, the Choctaw learned how to grow corn. At last, they could plant crops that they could eat year-round. Corn could be used in many ways, either fresh as cobs and kernels, or ground into flour or cornmeal. The traveling life became a thing of the past. People settled in villages and created strong communities.

Eventually there were about 50 Choctaw villages. They were scattered across parts of southeast Mississippi, southwestern Alabama, southeast Louisiana, and Florida. This part of the country provided dense forests full of game, rolling hills with fertile soil, and a climate with just the right blend of sunshine and rain. The villages were built near major rivers, such as the Pearl, the Tombigbee, and the Pascagoula. A few of the larger villages had moats around them for protection. Others had palisades, or reinforced walls, to keep enemies out.

Many of the Choctaw villages had palisades surrounding them. These walls made it harder for raiding tribes or curious explorers to attack.

Some villages had only 100 or so people living in them, but some numbered over 1,000. A chief ran each village. He was always a respected member of the tribe. He had a council of elders who helped him make decisions for the village. They would decide what to plant or if they should go to war with another tribe.

The Choctaw traded their goods with other tribes in the area, including the Quapaw and the Chickasaw. They often traded their corn and other goods, such as beaver and bear pelts, for seashells, pearls, and copper. They used these items to decorate their clothing.

In the 1500s, Hernando de Soto led a group of Spanish explorers to Indian territory. They were searching for a fabled land of youth and riches. As they searched for their treasures, they made a number of demands on the Choctaw tribe. They wanted to take servants, canoes, and women.[1] The Spaniards took a hostage: the Choctaw chief Tuscaloosa. They said they would free him only if the Choctaw gave them what they wanted. Tuscaloosa escaped, and the Choctaw fought the Spanish in the village of Mabila. In the end, thousands of Choctaw died, but only a handful of Spaniards were killed.[2]

Although the Spaniards left soon after the battle, Europeans returned to Choctaw territory in the late 1600s. This time they came from France and Great Britain. They traded guns, knives, axes, and cooking pots for Choctaw

During the battle, de Soto burned the village of Mabila.

corn and deerskins. The Europeans also brought sickness with them. The diseases ripped through the tribe, and thousands more Choctaw died.

As the eighteenth century began, both France and Great Britain fought to control trade with the Indians. The Choctaw decided to ally with France. Great Britain was angry. In 1711, the British gathered 1,700 Native Americans from the Creek and Chickasaw tribes to battle the Choctaw. When the skirmish ended, 200 Choctaw were dead, and hundreds more had been taken as slaves. Eventually, the British gained control. They kicked the French out of the territory.

A Time of Treaties

During the early 1800s, the Choctaw signed a number of treaties with the

A memorial marking the Treaty of Dancing Rabbit Creek was erected in September 1929.

U.S. government. With almost every treaty, the Choctaw lost more land. Millions of acres throughout Mississippi were signed over to the U.S. government. In exchange, the Choctaw received fewer acres in Oklahoma. Slowly the Choctaw were edged out of their homelands and forced to move west.

In 1830, President Andrew Jackson signed the Indian Removal Act. It stated that all tribes east of the Mississippi River had to move west of the river. Several Choctaw leaders met with U.S. officials. They agreed to move, and signed the Treaty of Dancing Rabbit Creek. Almost 20,000

Choctaw had to decide where to go. Most of them chose to head to Oklahoma.

The Choctaw were one of the first groups to make the 500-mile walk. Forced to move right away, they left during the harsh winter of 1831. The journey was so brutal that it became known as the Trail of Tears. Thousands of marchers died from starvation, illness, the cold, and exhaustion.

Life in Oklahoma

At last the long trek was over. The Choctaw worked to create a new way of life in Oklahoma. They built farms near rivers. They cut down trees and built homes, churches, and schools. Instead

Although this cartoon makes President Jackson look like a caring father to the Native Americans, the difference between his size and theirs tells a different story. It shows that Jackson—and the U.S.—saw Indians as inferior.

of growing corn, they learned to grow a new crop: wheat. They also began raising cattle and other types of livestock. They tried hard to start over in the new land, but it was not easy. Many people were poor and ill, as health care was impossible to find. In 1838, the Choctaw wrote a new constitution.

In 1898, the Choctaw Nation senate gathered at the capitol building in Tuskahoma, Oklahoma.

They updated it in 1842, 1850, and 1860. They also created a court system and set their capital in Tuskahoma.

Unfortunately, their troubles were not over. When the United States fought in the Civil War (1861–1865), both the North and the South wanted Native American support. The Choctaw joined the South, largely because they lived in southern states. Some of them were also slave owners. When the North won the war, the U.S. government punished the Choctaw. It took back large parts of their western territory.

In 1869, the Transcontinental Railroad finally joined the eastern and western halves of the country. Suddenly people from all across the nation were coming to Choctaw territory, hoping to build homes and plant crops. Many of these homesteaders, as they were called, built their farms on Native American lands. Meanwhile, oil was discovered in Oklahoma. More people flooded into the area, this time looking for fortune.

Righting a Few Wrongs

During World War I (1914–1918), many Native Americans, including Choctaws, joined the U.S. Military. Near the end of the war, the Choctaw worked as code talkers. These soldiers sent telephone messages in their native language to keep them secret from the enemy. Legend has it that a Choctaw named Albert Billy was the first one to suggest using the Native

American language to pass military secrets. Supposedly, one night a German general was captured. His only request was to be told "what nationality was on the phones that night." The answer? "Just Americans."[4]

In 1924, the U.S. passed the Indian Citizenship Act. It granted the rights of citizenship to all Native Americans born in the United States.

Dr. Joseph Dixon believed in this change. He wrote, "The Indian, though a man without a country, the Indian who has suffered a thousand wrongs considered the white man's burden and from mountains, plains, and divides, the Indian threw himself into the struggle." In other words, the Native Americans were willing to fight for the United States, even though they had been through many hardships. Their service earned them the right to citizenship.

The Choctaw code talkers made it possible to share important secrets without worrying that the enemy would intercept them and understand the details.

In July 1970, President Richard Nixon made lasting changes in the country's relationship with Native Americans. He called his new policy "self-determination without termination"—self-government without end.

The U.S. government began changing other policies affecting Native Americans. In 1934, the Indian Reorganization Act was passed. It decreased the federal government's role in Indian affairs and provided money to help develop better health care and education. It also returned some land to Native Americans.

Several decades later, in 1975, Congress passed the Indian Self-Determination and Education Assistance Act. This allowed the Choctaw, and other tribes, to set up their own governments. They could make contracts with the U.S. government, and they could build their own schools. These new freedoms allowed the Choctaw to preserve their language, customs, and beliefs.

From their early days of planting corn to their days of raising cattle, from being forced to leave to being allowed to self-govern, the Choctaw have been a close community. No matter where they have lived, they have respected their traditions and fought to keep them alive.

Spirit Dogs

Hernando de Soto reaches the Mississippi River.

In October 1540, Hernando de Soto and his group of explorers arrived in Choctaw territory. They were riding on the backs of mysterious "spirit dogs." These animals were actually a type of pony that soon became vital to the Choctaw way of life. The ponies were used for traveling, hunting, and farming. Ropes, saddles, or reins were rarely needed. Although they were small, they were some of the toughest, hardest-working, and gentlest horses in existence.

Three hundred years later, the Choctaw were forced to march the Trail of Tears. Choctaw ponies traveled with them. Writer John Fusco described when a Choctaw woman spotted one of the ponies along the trail. "In a blizzard she spotted one of the small Choctaw ponies carrying five children on its back at once," he wrote. "He had been a partner in the good hunting days and he was with them now, in times of hardship on a long strange road."[5]

Thousands of Choctaw people died along the Trail of Tears. Many ponies did, too. Knowing how much these animals meant to the Native Americans, the U.S. government rounded up and killed most of the ponies. The Choctaw pony was nearly extinct, until a few people decided to protect them. Thanks to them, the ponies are still here today. As Fusco writes, "Perhaps a society that has finally come to value sacred sites along with national landmarks will someday come to recognize this big-hearted little horse as a historical and cultural treasure."[6]

Horses made life much faster and easier for the Choctaw. They were used for everyday work and travel, and for hunting buffalo.

CHAPTER 3
CRADLEBOARDS AND CRAFTS

Traditionally, Choctaw men served as chiefs and councilmen. They fished and hunted game, including bear, deer, bison, wild turkeys, rabbits, and otters. They made tools and weapons, such as axes, tomahawks, and knives. They built homes and canoes. They played stickball. But it was the women who were in charge. The women made sure the village and its people survived from day to day.

The Choctaw Nation has traditionally been a matriarchal society. This means women governed the community, and mothers were the head of the family. Although men hunted game, the women usually dressed the animals, and then put the meat, hide, and bones to use. Men cleared the land for crops and, using sharp sticks, dug holes for the seeds. Women harvested the plants and turned the produce into food. They stored much of it for leaner times. Women also spent hours picking fruits, nuts, and berries, as more than half of the Choctaws' diet was made up of what grew, not what was hunted. Women also prepared the animal hides for use as clothing and blankets. They used the animals' claws, teeth, and bones for jewelry and tools. At the same time, women took care of the home. They sewed clothing, taught the children, and made

Pack baskets were much like today's backpacks. They carried food, drink, and even children.

wares such as baskets, pottery, and beading.

Home, Sweet Home

Choctaw homes were made from materials at hand. Most families had a summer home and a winter home. The summer homes were made from loosely woven reeds that allowed fresh, cool air to come inside. Winter homes, on the other hand, were made of tree saplings woven tightly together. The cracks were sealed with a mix of clay and grass. This helped keep the cold air out. Standing posts buried in the ground kept the house strong during heavy rains or winds.

Both types of homes had thatched grass or bark-shingled roofs. One or two holes in the roof let out the smoke from cooking fires. Their single doors were often quite small, rarely higher than four feet tall. Adults coming in or out would have to duck or hit their head.

The interior of Choctaw homes had simple furniture. Platforms made from woven reeds or river cane were used for everything from a bed or table to a seat or shelf. Animal skins were used as blankets.[1]

This home has river cane walls and a grass thatched roof for the hot summer months.

The Choctaw Family

Weddings were exciting events in Choctaw villages. Most of the time, the bride and groom came from different villages or districts. Once married, they lived together, but getting divorced was pretty simple. If the wife decided it was not working out, she would put all of her husband's belongings outside on the ground. That was the signal that the marriage was over.[2] She kept the home and the children, and the husband returned to his family.

Childbirth was a quiet, private event for Choctaw women. They would go away for a few hours once labor started, and then come back to introduce the baby to the rest of the tribe.

Babies were usually named after something the mother saw while she was giving birth, a large tribal event, or a specific characteristic. Later, that name would change to reflect adulthood.

The baby was often carried on a cradleboard. This flat board was made of a smooth piece of wood or woven basket fibers. It was typically painted or decorated with beads. Soft moss or animal fur made it comfortable for the baby. Wrapped in blankets, the baby would be strapped to the board with leather ties or other cords. When the mother needed her hands free, she would lean the board against a

Cradleboards allowed mothers to do their many chores and still keep a close eye on their babies.

wall or tree, strap it onto her back, or tie it to the side of a horse. The baby would be safe and in sight.[3]

Some babies spent time in their cradleboards with pieces of wood or bags of sand on their foreheads. This flattened their foreheads, but did not cause any damage or pain. For the Choctaw, a flattened forehead was considered very attractive. When they were older, boys and men might get tattoos or pierce their noses.

Taking care of the children was the job of the mother—not the father. If a male was needed to teach lessons or do any training, one of the mother's brothers was called in instead. Boys spent much of their days wrestling, participating in archery contests, and playing strategy games under the direction of their uncles. Boys were not considered men until they proved themselves in hunting, stickball, or battle.[4]

Choctaw arrows were used for hunting. They were made out of several different materials, including deer antlers and animal bones. V-shaped wooden fishing sticks were used to catch fish.

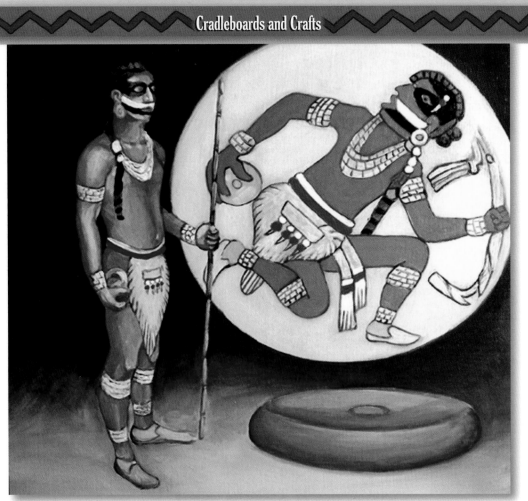

Chunkey was one of the Choctaws' favorite games. It required good aim and a strong throwing arm.

Children were expected to help with chores, but there was a lot of time for fun too. Dice games using corn kernels or fruit seeds were a popular way to play. Another fun game was chunkey. A smooth round disk made of stone or clay was rolled along the ground. Just as the disk started to wobble—but before it fell down—players threw long poles at it. The one who came closest to actually touching the stone was declared the winner.[5]

Making Tools and Other Goods

The Choctaw used the river cane, or *i-hi*, that grew along creek banks for many purposes. The women took long pieces of the cane and wove them into mats, some as large as six feet square. These mats were put to use in

Weaving baskets from river cane was practical. It also gave the Native Americans a way to create pleasing patterns and designs.

many ways, from bedding and wall hangings to funeral blankets. In addition, women used the river cane to make a variety of baskets.

Baskets were used in countless ways. They stored food, as well as carried it. Some were woven so tightly they could be used as bowls. Some baskets were even used to trap fish or game when hunting. While some of these baskets were plain, others had fancy designs. Many women would use dyes they made from flowers, roots, and bark to add color and create patterns. Basketry is a skill that is still practiced by Choctaw women. Their baskets are considered some of history's most prized treasures.

Kapucha Toli

Combining a stick with a ball to play a game is one of the oldest ideas in the world—just ask the Choctaw. They invented a game they call *kapucha toli*, or stickball. For these people, stickball was a serious game. In the past, tribes would play *kapucha toli* to settle conflicts, earning it the nickname "little brother of war."[6]

Each team had between 75 and 100 players. Each player held two sticks, or *kapucha*. These were used to pick up and carry a leather ball, or *towa*, to the goal, or *fabvssa*. The goal was a 12-foot-high post. The game had only one rule: no one could touch the ball with his hands. Otherwise, anything was allowed—kicking, tripping, and hitting. Injuries were common.

Bill EagleRoad III of the Oklahoma Choctaw Nation described the game in an article for *Indian Country*. "[The game] was used as an alternate to war. So if you had a dispute over any kind of resource or land, food, water, or hunting grounds, maybe you would settle the feuds with this game. . . . And back then, they didn't have any rules really. The only rules were that you had to use your sticks to get a ball and hit a pole."[7]

Stickball is still played among the Choctaw, although there are a few more rules now. While no one wears any helmets or padding, there are rules about how and where players can strike each other. "We do our best," says EagleRoad. "But it's like football, you can do only so much to prevent injuries. And you don't want to lose the original identity of the game."[8]

Choctaw, Mississippi, is still home to the World Series of Stickball, which is played as part of the annual Choctaw Indian Fair.

For the Choctaw, stickball meant far more than just a game. It settled arguments and helped tribes avoid going to war.

This painting by George Catlin shows the Choctaw performing the annual Eagle Dance. It was done in honor of the War Eagle, the bird that won all battles over others. The men's heads were often decorated in eagle tail feathers.

CHAPTER 4
SONGS AND SPIRITS

The Choctaw life was full of music. Singing and dancing were part of every gathering, from celebrations to funerals. Special dances were created for the birth of a baby, weddings, and sending men off to hunt. The dances were not short, either. Some started at sundown and ran until sunrise. Everyone was invited to join in.

War dances were serious events. Warriors would prepare to fight by rubbing their bodies with herbs. These were believed to bring them strength and courage. Many would also mark their faces with red, white, or black paint. The men put eagle feathers in their hair and danced around spears that were stuck in the ground. Women joined in this dance.

Warriors would sing before being killed by an enemy. Medicine men would sing in order to please the spirits and heal their patients. Instruments often accompanied songs and dances. Sticks were banged together and drums kept the beat going. Some of the Choctaw rang bells or blew whistles. Others learned to play an *uskala*. This flute was made of hollow tubes of cane. It was also played to welcome visitors and to announce the start of an attack during battle.[1]

For decades, the Choctaw have celebrated good corn harvests by dancing and giving thanks to the spirits for their generosity.

One of the most important celebrations for the Choctaw is the Green Corn Ceremony, held in late July. Lucy Cherry, a Choctaw, was born in 1869. She wrote about a ceremony she witnessed. "Preparations began a week before the event, with men hunting deer, squirrels, and bear, and killing hogs and cattle; green corn was also harvested from the fields. The families gathered up the food they had obtained, along with many of the household furnishings and headed for the Dance Grounds."[2] The ceremony lasted four days, and every part of the festival focused on thanking the spirits for a good harvest. By the early 1900s, because of their forced removal west and struggle to adapt to a new lifestyle, the Choctaw stopped celebrating the Green Corn Ceremony. It finally returned in the 1970s. Today, the dance is held annually again and is part of the Choctaw Indian Fair.

Deerskin Clothing

Like many other Native American groups, the Choctaw used every part of the animals they hunted. The meat was used as food. The hides were turned into clothing, shoes, and blankets. Deerskin was used to make men's breechcloths, as well as women's wraparound skirts. Neither men nor women tended to wear shirts unless the weather was wet or cool. Then they added a poncho-style cape.

Beaded, painted moccasins were made out of animal pelts, although most of the tribe went barefoot until the weather turned cold. During winter months, people added deerskin leggings to keep their legs warm, plus shawls or fur robes.

The bones, teeth, and claws of animals were often used as farming or hunting tools. Some were added to clothing and necklaces, earrings, and bracelets. Both men and women wore their hair quite long. Girls tended to fashion combs out of seashells, antler pieces, copper, beads, and flowers.

The Choctaw carved combs from antlers.

Good and Evil

While the Choctaw people liked to wear jewelry, it was not always done just for decoration. Some of the pieces were charms or amulets, worn to protect a person from evil spirits. The tribe believed that spirits were in control of everything that happened, and that these spirits could be found in people, animals, and nature.

A person's inner spirit was known as *shilup*, or "shadow." A person's outer spirit was called its *shilombish*. The Choctaw believed that dreams were what happened when the outer spirit left the person's body while he was sleeping. Missionaries came to Choctaw territory in the early nineteenth century to teach the Indians Christianity. Many of the Choctaw were not convinced. They continued to believe in their traditional spirits and the power of the supernatural.[3]

Medicine men and women often sang and danced to the spirits in order to bring healing. They gave people who were sick pouches filled with herbs, along with sacred objects such as a pipe or rattle. The people also prayed to spirits to ask for a good harvest and to give thanks. Sometimes these ceremonies would last several weeks.

Dancing and singing were part of religious ceremonies. The Choctaw believed that the spirits would help them if they prayed with song.

When a Choctaw died, a dog or pony was sometimes sacrificed at the same time. This would give the deceased a companion for the trip to the afterworld.

The Bone Pickers

When a member of the tribe died, both the inner spirit and outer spirit left the body. The Choctaw believed the *shilombish* would stay on earth for up to several months before finally making the trek to the Land of Ghosts. Following the death, the body was washed and dressed. Then, it was usually put inside a small cabin that was placed on tall poles, about six feet off the ground, to keep it safe from animals. Some of the person's most treasured items were added to the cabin for use in the afterworld. For men, this was often a weapon, such as a bow and arrows. For women, it was sometimes a cooking pot, basket, or piece of jewelry. The family had time to gather, cry, and sing to their loved one. People would give speeches honoring the person and his or her accomplishments.[4]

The mourning period usually lasted for four months. When it was over, it was time for the bone pickers. These honored tribal members had long fingernails on their thumbs, forefingers, and middle fingers. They would use

While the bone pickers did their job, family would often come to mourn. They held the bones and helped carry them back to the village's bone house.

them to peel the remaining flesh from the bones of the deceased. The flesh was buried or burned, and the bones were washed. The skull was painted red, and the bones were all placed in a box and given to the family. A huge feast followed, and then the box of bones was placed in the bone house, next to the bones of other family members.

Choctaw funerals began changing in the early 1800s after missionaries came to the area. More European-style funerals took place, with the body being placed in a cemetery. The Choctaw still practiced some old traditions, however. They were not about to give up their heritage.

Pushmataha and Peter Pitchlynn

Pushmataha

Two of the best-known leaders of the Choctaw people were Pushmataha (1764?–1824) and Peter Pitchlynn (1806–1881).

By the time Pushmataha was a teenager, people knew who he was. He was one of the best stickball players around, and he was a successful warrior. As an adult, he met a number of men who helped him come to respect white Americans. Soon, Pushmataha became an expert negotiator. By 1805, he had become a Choctaw chief. When the British asked the Choctaw and other tribes to join them against the Americans, Pushmataha spoke out against it. His speech was so well done that one reporter wrote he had "never [heard a speaker] who had such music in his tones, such energy in his manner and such power over his audience as Pushmataha."[5]

Throughout his life, Pushmataha did all he could to maintain peace for the Native Americans. He fought beside President Andrew Jackson, who called him "the greatest and bravest Indian" he had ever met. When he died, the Choctaw's gravestone read, "Pushmataha was a warrior of great distinction. He was wise in council, eloquent in an extraordinary degree, and on all occasions, and under all circumstances, the white man's friend."[6]

Peter Pitchlynn was the son of John Pitchlynn—one of the men who had convinced Pushmataha to support the Americans. Peter's mother was a Choctaw. His father was a white trader. After Andrew Jackson had moved most of the Choctaw west, Pitchlynn helped create a national school system for the children. He often went to Washington, D.C., as a Choctaw delegate. He stood against any threat to tribal lands, and he did all he could to make sure the federal government left the Choctaw Nation alone.[7]

Peter Pitchlynn

In July 2015, President Barack Obama visited the Choctaw Nation of Oklahoma to talk to the youth. He spoke about several new programs that would help young people "achieve their potential not just for the benefit of themselves and their communities, but for our entire nation."[1]

CHAPTER 5
FACING THE FUTURE

On August 9, 2016, the town of Clayton, Oklahoma, opened a grocery store owned by the Choctaw Nation. It was the first of what the Choctaw Nation hoped would be several stores. "It is a part of the vision of this council," Chief Gary Batton told *Indian Country*.

Clayton is a tiny town, with only 1,000 residents. The closest grocery store was 50 miles away. The Choctaw in the area knew something had to be done. "They [members of the council] want to make sure that our smaller communities thrive and do well," Chief Batton continued. "Without this, I don't know if Clayton would be here 20 years from now. This is making sure we keep Clayton alive, growing and prospering."[2]

In addition to offering fresh produce, groceries, a butcher shop, and a fueling station, the new store was hoping to become a place for friends to meet and share a cup of coffee. It has a 45-seat dining area, and the walls are covered in murals showing the rich Choctaw heritage.

The store also planned to be a place for people to go during severe weather. "One of the things we did do was put enough backup power in the store that no matter what happens from mother nature, the store will remain open," explained Tim Locke, Choctaw Country Market Manager.[3]

In 1949, the Inter-Tribal Council of the Five Civilized Tribes was formed. The council cooperated with European settlers, trading with them and learning their languages. Since then, these five tribes decided to work together as one unit, supporting each other. In 2016, the following leaders made up the council (left to right): Governor Bill Anoatubby, Chickasaw Nation; Principal Chief Leonard Harjo, Seminole Nation; Principal Chief James Floyd, Muscogee (Creek) Nation; Chief Gary Batton, Choctaw Nation; and Principal Chief Bill John Baker, Cherokee Nation.

The Choctaw Today

The Choctaw is the third largest tribe in the United States. It has nearly 200,000 members. Almost half of them still live throughout parts of Oklahoma.[4] The rest tend to live in Mississippi, Alabama, and Louisiana. Although today's Choctaw have adapted many of the modern ways of life, they also hold on to many of their traditions. Since the Indian Reorganization Act of 1934, all Native American tribes have been able to set up their own governments. The Choctaw Nation of both Oklahoma and Mississippi have their own constitutions in place. They are governed by a tribal council.

The Choctaw Nation of Oklahoma focuses on keeping its culture's rituals and heritage alive. Their language is taught both online and in 35 high schools and three colleges. They have a tribal newspaper called *Bishinik*. Each spring, members come together to honor those lost on the Trail of Tears, and there are yearly gatherings called powwows. The Oklahoma and Mississippi groups operate a number of casinos as well.

Smaller groups of Choctaw live in other states. The Jena band lives in Louisiana and has several hundred members. About 6,000 Choctaw make up the MOWA (of Mobile and Washington counties) band in southwestern Alabama. No matter the size of these groups, all work to honor their heritage and to carry those ideas and beliefs into the future.

Logo for the Jena band of Choctaw

The Annual Choctaw Indian Fair

Dancing at the Annual Choctaw Indian Fair

Since 1949, the city of Choctaw, Mississippi, has hosted the annual Choctaw Indian Fair. For four days, fairgoers can "celebrate our heritage and share our beautiful and vibrant culture." All ages are welcome. Events include cultural displays, social dancing, carnival rides, tribal arts, live music, and traditional Choctaw food. People enjoy watching the stickball competition. They cheer for their favorite players in the men's, women's, youth (14 to17 years old), and young people's (10 to 13 years old) games.[5]

Many people also enjoy the Indian Princess Pageant. The young lady who is chosen as the winner serves as an ambassador for the Choctaw tribe for a full year. Contestants are judged in five categories: talent, formal dress, traditional dress, question and answer, and interview. Former princess MeShay LeAnn Jimmie told WTOK, "I get to travel to different places, and talk to other people, and represent my tribe as well, and let them know who I am as the Mississippi Band of Choctaw Indians."[6]

For serious athletes, there are two exciting competitions: the Rez Run and the Iron Warrior. In the Rez Run, runners race along trails through the fairgrounds. Routes vary from one mile to 5K and 10K. Iron Warriors compete in strength challenges. They might pull or carry extremely heavy loads or lift huge tires.

900 CE	The Choctaw begin to farm corn. They build villages.
1540	Hernando de Soto leads Spanish explorers into what is now Alabama.
1825	The first Choctaw constitution is ratified. Four years later, the Mississippi legislature declares it invalid.
1830	President Andrew Jackson signs the Indian Removal Act on May 28. The Choctaw sign the Treaty of Dancing Rabbit Creek in September.
1831	Thousands of Native Americans begin marching west. So many people die on the journey, it becomes known as the Trail of Tears.
1838	In Oklahoma, the Choctaw write a new constitution. It will be updated several times over the next 25 years. They create a court system.
1859	Oil is discovered in Oklahoma.
1861	The Choctaw fight for the Confederacy in the U.S. Civil War.
1869	The Transcontinental Railroad connects the United States from the East Coast to the West Coast.
1883	The Choctaw capital is moved to Tuskahoma, Oklahoma.
1914–1918	Many Choctaw fight for the United States in World War I.
1924	The U.S. passes the Indian Citizenship Act. It grants the rights of citizenship to all Native Americans born in the United States.
1934	The Indian Reorganization Act decreases federal control over Indian affairs.
1941–1945	During World War II, the Choctaw work as code talkers.
1975	Congress passes the Indian Self-Determination and Education Assistance Act.
1981	The U.S. government declares the 1860 Choctaw constitution as valid.
1987	The Choctaw Nation opens its first casino.
1990	The Choctaw Nation opens its first travel plaza.
2006	Leaders of the Five Civilized Tribes (Cherokee, Chickasaw, Choctaw, Creek, and Seminole) celebrate the centennial of the Five Civilized Tribes Act of 1906. This act allowed these particular tribes to govern themselves.
2016	The Choctaw Nation opens the first of a chain of grocery stores in Clayton, Oklahoma.

Nation	Choctaw
Name meaning	"People of Chahta," a famous Choctaw leader
Culture area	American South
Geography	Mississippi, Louisiana, Alabama, and Oklahoma
Homes	Summer: reeds; winter: mud
Main livestock	Sheep, cattle
Main crops	Corn, squash, wheat, beans, sunflowers
Experts	Weaving cane baskets, beadwork
Population, 2016	198,835
Primary revenue	Travel plazas and casinos
Language	Choctaw: taught online and offered in 35 high schools and 3 colleges

Chapter 1
1. "The Choctaw Blowgun." *Chahta Anumpa Aiikhvna School of Choctaw Language.*
2. Ibid.
3. Ibid.
4. Vocabulary in Native American Languages: "Choctaw Words." *Native Languages of the Americas.*

Chapter 2
1. "Choctaw Indians." TSHA Texas State Historical Association.
2. "Mabila: The Battle between Hernando de Soto and Chief Tascalusa." *About Education.* April 9, 2016.
3. "1924 Indian Citizenship Act." Nebraska Studies.
4. "Choctaw Indians." Indians.org.
5. John Fusco, "The Choctaw Indian Pony: An Endangered Treasure." *Women & Horses Magazine*, March/April 2006.
6. Ibid.

Chapter 3
1. "Native American Homes." *Native Languages of the Americas.*
2. Donna L. Akers, *Culture and Customs of the Choctaw Indians* (Santa Barbara, Calif: Greenwood, 2013), p. 83.
3. "Native American Cradleboards." Native Languages.
4. "The Role of Choctaw Fathers and Uncles." *Chahta Anumpa Aiikhvna/ School of Choctaw Language.*
5. "Choctaw Games." Choctaw Nation.
6. Joey McWilliams, "Choctaw Stickball: A Game of History, Passion and Pride," Indian Country, July 2, 2015.
7. Ibid.
8. Ibid.

Chapter 4
1. "The Choctaw River Cane Flute." *Chahta Anumpa Aiikhvna/School of Choctaw Language.*
2. "Green Corn Ceremony." *Chahta Anumpa Aiikhvna/School of Choctaw Language.*
3. "Ancient Choctaw Burial Practice." *Chahta Anumpa Aiikhvna/School of Choctaw Language.*
4. Ibid.
5. "Pushmataha." *American National Biography Online.*
6. Ibid.
7. "Pitchlynn, Peter Perkins." Oklahoma Historical Society.

Chapter 5
1. Tyler Jones, " 'Halito, Mr. President'— President Obama Visits Choctaw Nation of Oklahoma." *Native News Online*, July 16, 2015.
2. Staff, "First Choctaw Grocery Store Opens its Doors." *Indian Country*, August 11, 2016.
3. Marissa Budzynski, "Choctaw Nation Market Brings Fresh Food to Rural Areas," KXII News 12, August 16, 2016.
4. "Choctaw Nation Top 10 Fast Facts."
5. "Choctaw Indian Fair."
6. Candace Barnette, "Preserving Choctaw Culture: Princess Pageant," WTOK, July 10, 2014.

Works Consulted

"1924 Indian Citizenship Act." Nebraska Studies. http://www. nebraskastudies.org/0700/frameset_reset.html?http://www. nebraskastudies.org/0700/stories/0701_0146.html

Akers, Donna L. *Culture and Customs of the Choctaw Indians*. Santa Barbara, California: Greenwood, 2013.

Barnette, Candace. "Preserving Choctaw Culture: Princess Pageant." WTOK, July 10, 2014. http://www.wtok.com/home/headlines/ Preserving-Choctaw-Culture-Princess-Pageant-266673511.html

Chahta Anumpa Aiikhvna School of Choctaw Language. http://www. choctawschool.com/galleries/chahta-anumpa-aiikhvna.aspx

"Choctaw Games." *Choctaw Nation*. https://www.choctawnation.com/ history-culture/choctaw-traditions/choctaw-games

"Choctaw Indian Fair." http://www.choctawindianfair.com/index.html

"Choctaw Indians." Indians.org. http://www.indians.org/articles/ choctaw-indians.html

"Choctaw Indians." *TSHA Texas State Historical Association*. https:// tshaonline.org/handbook/online/articles/bmc57

"Choctaw Nation Top 10 Fast Facts." http://s3.amazonaws.com/ choctaw-msldigital/assets/350/Fast_Facts_original.pdf

Fusco, John. *The Choctaw Indian Pony: An Endangered Treasure. Women & Horses Magazine*, March/April 2006. http:// returntofreedom.org/wp-content/uploads/2014/11/choctaw-article.pdf

The Inter-Tribal Council of the Five Civilized Tribes. http://www. fivecivilizedtribes.org

Jena Band of Choctaw Indians. http://www.jenachoctaw.org

Jones, Tyler. " 'Halito, Mr. President'—President Obama Visits Choctaw Nation of Oklahoma." *Native News Online*, July 16, 2015. http://nativenewsonline.net/currents/halito-mr-president- president-obama-visits-choctaw-nation-of-oklahoma/

Mabila: The Battle between Hernando de Soto and Chief Tascalusa." *About Education*, April 9, 2016. http://archaeology.about.com/od/ mameterms/qt/Mabila.htm

McWilliams, Joey. "Choctaw Stickball: A Game of History, Passion and Pride." *Indian Country*, July 2, 2015. http://indiancountrytodaymedianetwork.com/2015/07/02/choctaw-stickball-game-history-passion-and-pride-160940

Native Languages.org http://www.native-languages.org/

"Pitchlynn, Peter Perkins.' Oklahoma Historical Society http://www.anb.org/articles/20/20-00828.html

Vocabulary in Native American Languages: Choctaw Words. Native Languages of the Americas. http://www.native-languages.org/choctaw_words.htm

On the Internet

Ducksters: Native Americans for Kids
http://www.ducksters.com/history/native_americans.php

History for Kids: Native Americans
http://www.historyforkids.net/native-americans.html

Mr. Donn: Native Americans, "Choctaw"
http://nativeamericans.mrdonn.org/southeast/choctaw.html

Further Reading

Bowes, John P. *The Choctaw*. New York: Chelsea House, 2010.

De Capua, Sarah. *The Choctaw*. New York: Marshall Cavendish, 2009.

Gray-Kanatilosh, Barbara A. *Choctaw*. Minneapolis, MN: Abdo Publishing Company, 2007.

Quinlivan, Ada. *Choctaw*. New York: PowerKids Press, 2016.

Sonneborn, Liz. *The Choctaws*. Mankato, MN: Lerner Publications, 2007.

Tingle, Tim. *Crossing Bok Chitto: A Choctaw Take of Friendship and Freedom*. El Paso, TX; Cinco Puntos Press, 2008.

Tingle, Tim. *How I Became a Ghost: A Choctaw Trail of Tears Story*. Oklahoma City, OK: Roadrunner Press, 2015.

ambassador (am-BAS-uh-der)—A representative of a government or group.

amulet (AM-yoo-let)—A sacred object worn to provide protection.

archery (AR-chur-ee)—The use of a bow to shoot arrows.

casino (kuh-SEE-noh)—A gambling business.

fertile (FER-tul)—Rich or healthy, as of farmland.

matriarchal (may-tree-AR-kul)—Run or ruled by the mothers of a society.

missionary (MIH-shuh-nayr-ee)—A person who travels to convert others to Christianity.

mural (MYUR-ul)—A large painting, usually done on a wall.

negotiator (neh-GOH-she-ay-tor)—A person who is good at helping two sides make a fair deal.

nomadic (noh-MAD-ik)—Constantly moving.

palisades (PAL-ih-saydz)—Reinforced walls built for protection.

scarcity (SKAYR-sih-tee)—A lack or shortage.

supernatural (soo-per-NAT-chrul)—Beyond scientific understanding.

MEET THE
AUTHOR

Tamra Orr is the author of more than 450 nonfiction books for readers of all ages. She lives in the Pacific Northwest with her husband and children. She graduated from Ball State University and has been writing ever since. When Orr is not researching and writing a book, she is writing letters, reading books, and camping in the incredibly beautiful state of Oregon.